A FROZEN WORLD

Published by Scholastic Australia in 2019.

Scholastic Australia Pty Limited
PO Box 579 Gosford NSW 2250
ABN 11 000 614 577
www.scholastic.com.au

Part of the Scholastic Group
Sydney • Auckland • New York • Toronto • London • Mexico City • New Delhi • Hong Kong • Buenos Aires • Puerto Rico

ISBN 978-1-74383-430-5

1 3 5 7 9 10 8 6 4 2

Written by Marilyn Easton
Designed by Nia Williams
Edited by Frankie Jones

Printed and bound in China.

A FROZEN WORLD

CONTENTS

INTRODUCTION

This is the charming Kingdom of Arendelle! The following pages explore this unique realm, from the bustling fjord to the towering North Mountain, including the royal castle – the heart of Arendelle, and home to Anna and Elsa. The castle is filled with many rooms from formal areas like the majestic great hall and the elegant portrait gallery to more casual spaces like Anna's bedroom and the cosy library. The detailed sections of every room offer a glimpse of what life is really like behind the castle walls. Excitement, magic and friends like Kristoff, Olaf and Sven are waiting just around the corner!

Outside the castle walls the friendly village of Arendelle awaits. In the village, visitors can find sweet-smelling flower shops and vendors offering Arendellian delicacies like lingonberry cream pie. A short distance from the bustle of the village sits Wandering Oaken's Trading Post and Sauna, where Oaken is always happy to chat about his latest invention. A bit farther lies Elsa's beautiful ice palace and the lush Valley of the Living Rock, where Grand Pabbie and the rest of Kristoff's troll family live.

Adventurers who dare journey farther north will encounter the mysterious Enchanted Forest – but first, they'll need to make it past the magical mist guarding the forest's entrance. Inside, Lieutenant Mattias, Yelana, Ryder and Honeymaren are waiting, but so are the spirits of nature – the Wind Spirit Gale, the Earth Giants, the Fire Spirit Bruni and the Water Nokk. The Kingdom of Arendelle and beyond holds exciting adventures for all who journey there!

ARENDELLE CASTLE

As one of the tallest buildings in the kingdom, Arendelle Castle is quite an impressive sight to behold. Complete with glittering turrets, intricate stained-glass windows and unique ice detailing provided by Elsa, this castle is fit for a queen. The outside of the castle is deeply connected to nature – it is both constructed with natural materials like wood and stone and surrounded by natural elements, from the majestic mountains to the crisp blue waters of the fjord.

Over the past several decades, Arendelle Castle has been home to the royal Arendelle family – a tradition that continues to this day with Anna and Elsa. During Anna and Elsa's childhoods, the gates to the castle were closed in order to hide Elsa's secret powers. Now the gates are open, welcoming townspeople and visitors from distant lands to enjoy the warmth, comfort and magic that can be found within the castle walls.

The sound of the bell being rung in the bell tower carries throughout the kingdom.

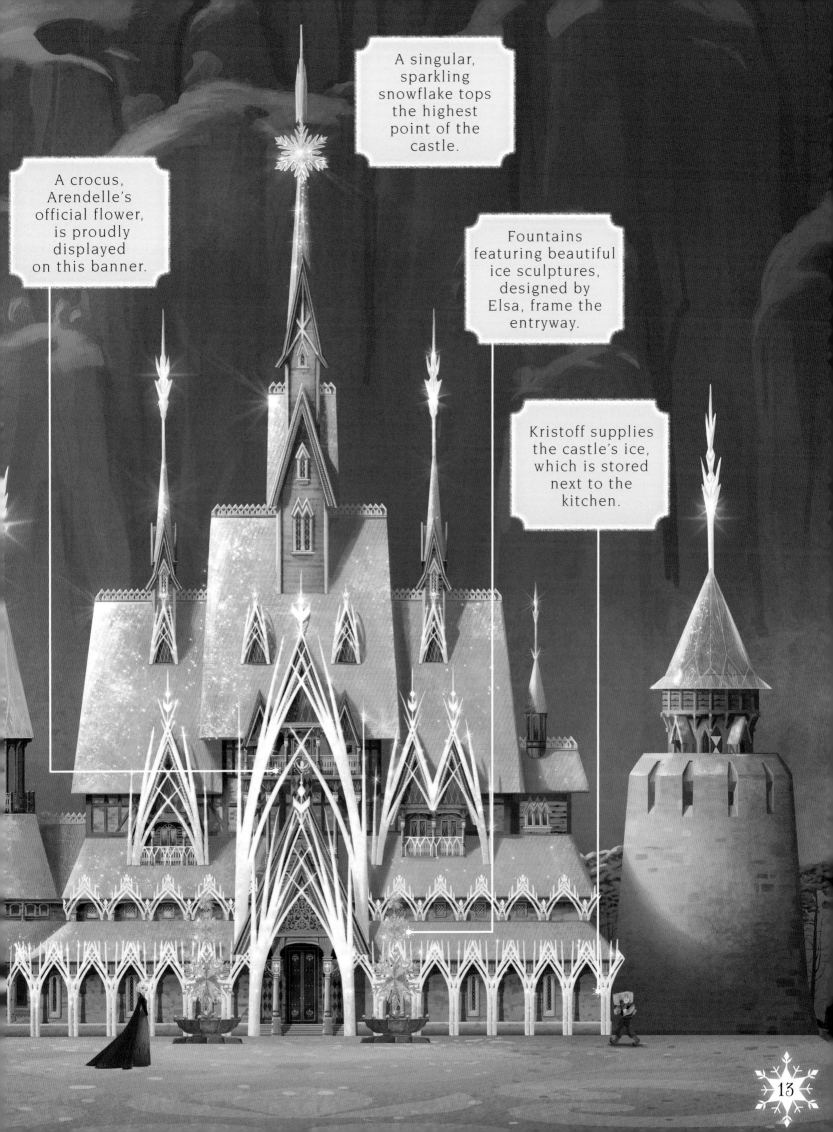

A singular, sparkling snowflake tops the highest point of the castle.

A crocus, Arendelle's official flower, is proudly displayed on this banner.

Fountains featuring beautiful ice sculptures, designed by Elsa, frame the entryway.

Kristoff supplies the castle's ice, which is stored next to the kitchen.

13

INSIDE ARENDELLE CASTLE

From cosy chambers to elegant halls, Arendelle Castle is a place of both excitement and comfort for Anna and Elsa. The castle used to be a lonely place for the royal sisters, but now that the gates have been re-opened, visitors are always stopping by with cheerful news and warm hugs. Outside of the main castle lies the chapel, a place for the community to gather, and the guard tower, which helps keep the people of Arendelle safe.

On a typical day, the main castle is where Anna and Elsa spend most of their time either savouring a good book or entertaining friends with a game of charades. Anna and Elsa enjoy spending time with each other and exploring their heritage in rooms like the portrait gallery and the library. The sisters also frequently visit the kitchen for a snack. The kitchen occupies almost the entire bottom floor of the castle – the cooks certainly need all of that room when they're preparing a grand feast!

Anna enjoys racing up the spiral staircase. Ready, set, go!

When someone borrows a book from the library, they must remember to return it!

If you're feeling artistic, visit the art supply room where you can express your creativity.

Stained-glass windows throughout the castle provide colourful light.

Elsa is preparing the great hall for a dance tonight.

Elsa

As a child, Elsa spent her days playing with her younger sister, Anna, throughout the castle halls. But Elsa was not an ordinary child, she had magical ice and snow powers! She shared her powers with her sister, until one day she accidentally struck Anna with her magic, which left a white streak in Anna's hair.

After that day, their concerned parents locked the castle gates and limited Elsa's contact with people. Her magic was getting too powerful – she had to conceal it from everyone, including Anna.

The castle doors did not reopen until coronation day when Elsa came of age to claim her right to the throne. It was a spirited celebration until Elsa's powers were exposed. She raced out of the castle, her powers turning the warm summer air into frigid winter. Fearing her powers may hurt someone, Elsa fled until she reached the North Mountain. There, she used her magical powers to create a dazzling ice palace.

Three years later, the Kingdom of Arendelle has returned to normal life (and normal weather). But recently a mysterious kulning sound has been calling to Elsa. Elsa responded to the call with her magic, but then her powers created a massive shock wave that shot across the fjord, which was answered by a light to the north. Now Elsa needs to journey north to find the source of the kulning sound, to save Arendelle and finally discover the truth about herself and her powers.

ANNA

After Elsa accidentally struck Anna with her powers, their parents rushed Anna to the Valley of the Living Rock where Grand Pabbie, the troll leader, removed all of her memories of Elsa's magic. Anna spent the rest of her childhood isolated from Elsa and the people of Arendelle. She spent each day inside the castle halls trying to find ways to pass the time, which included conversing with portraits and suits of armour – it was really quite lonely.

When Elsa's coronation finally approached, Anna was filled with excitement to finally have the castle doors open! But when Elsa fled from the castle, Anna felt responsible and went after her sister without hesitation. Though the journey was challenging, along the way Anna met her true love, Kristoff, and her new friends, Olaf and Sven.

Once she reached her sister, Anna was determined that she could convince Elsa to return to Arendelle and restore summer, but Elsa was still filled with doubt. Her fears consumed her and she accidentally struck Anna with her magic – this time in her heart. Through an act of true love, Anna was able to save her sister and herself. Summer returned to Arendelle and the castle doors remained opened for good.

Anna has spent the last three years making up for lost time with her sister, though recently she has had the feeling that Elsa is hiding something. Then, one night the natural elements suddenly leave Arendelle, threatening the lives of the villagers. Anna joins Elsa on her journey to find the source of the mysterious voice that's been calling to her and to save Arendelle.

Kristoff

Kristoff may seem a little rough around the edges, but deep inside he's a warm, caring friend – and a pretty decent lute player. Kristoff first met his true love, Anna, at Wandering Oaken's Trading Post and Sauna where he'd gone to pick up winter supplies and carrots for Sven, his best friend who also happens to be a reindeer.

Anna hired Kristoff and Sven to take her up the North Mountain to Elsa. At first, Kristoff refused since he was a bit of a loner, but with his ice harvesting business at a standstill thanks to unexpected wintry conditions, and Anna's persistence, he and Sven agreed. Soon the three were off on an adventure.

Along the way, they encountered a pack of dangerous wolves who chased them off a cliff, forcing Kristoff to abandon his sleigh mid-air and lose it in the process. As the group continued to overcome obstacles both natural and magical, Kristoff's knowledge of the surrounding forest and outdoor skills were essential.

As they spent more time together, Kristoff began to open his heart to Anna. When she was struck by Elsa's magic, he did everything in his power to help her recover. Once Anna was cured and summer returned to Arendelle, Elsa named Kristoff the official Arendelle Ice Master and Deliverer. Now, he spends his time mostly at the castle, with Anna and his friends, though he never goes too long between family visits to the Valley of the Living Rock.

SVEN

Kristoff's best friend and loyal companion Sven is a friend everyone can count on, though most days he could use a bath and a brushing. Sven requires little in life with the exception of a steady supply of his favourite snack – carrots – which he is always willing to share with Kristoff. Whether he's pulling a sleigh full of cargo, or carrying his friends on his back, his preferred speed is fast. But it isn't all snacks and sleighs for Sven – he's outrun a pack of wolves, jumped across a snowy cliff and fallen into dangerous icy waters. No matter what challenges he encounters, Sven remains optimistic and knows Kristoff always has his back. Although he will always hold a place in his heart for the wilderness, Sven quickly adapted to life in Arendelle, mostly thanks to the constant supply of carrots.

OLAF

Olaf is a young, imaginative snowman who was magically created by Elsa for her and Anna to play with when they were children. When Grand Pabbie removed Anna's memories of Elsa's powers, her memory of Olaf vanished as well. But when Elsa unleashed her powers on the North Mountain, Olaf was brought to life. He met Anna, Kristoff and Sven on their journey up the North Mountain to find Elsa and he's been a part of their adventures ever since.

Thanks to Elsa permafrosting Olaf, he was finally able to experience summer – without melting! Now that he's discovered the mystery of what snow does in summer, Olaf is learning even more fascinating facts about the world, and has even learned how to read. His latest discovery is that water has a memory. Every day holds a new adventure for Olaf and he appreciates each moment, especially when he's spending time with his best friends.

WHO'S WHO
ARENDELLE CASTLE

GERDA knows everything about Arendelle Castle because she has lived there even longer than Anna and Elsa have! Having cared for them since they were born, she shares a special bond with the sisters. When they were children, Gerda always made sure their birthdays were special and would sneak them chocolate treats from the kitchen every now and again.

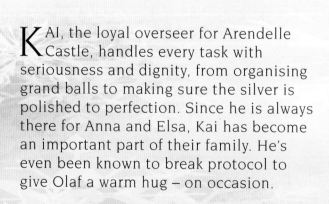

KAI, the loyal overseer for Arendelle Castle, handles every task with seriousness and dignity, from organising grand balls to making sure the silver is polished to perfection. Since he is always there for Anna and Elsa, Kai has become an important part of their family. He's even been known to break protocol to give Olaf a warm hug – on occasion.

HANS initially presents himself as a charming prince from the Southern Isles, but his motives are purely devious. As the youngest of 13 brothers, Hans would have to marry a queen in order to rule a kingdom. His quest for power was revealed when he declined to save Anna's life. After Anna saved herself, she promptly exiled Hans from Arendelle.

OLINA and her staff prepare three meals – plus snacks – for the entire castle every day! From elegant five-tiered cakes worthy of a royal feast to Sven's favourite crunchy crispy carrot snacks, Olina has every recipe memorised and cooks all of her creations from the heart – that's why they taste so good!

THE DUKE OF WESELTON, a weasel-like royal with bird-like dance moves, was one of the visitors at Arendelle Castle during Elsa's coronation. When her powers were revealed, the Duke quickly jumped to the conclusion that Elsa was a monster. Due to his unapologetic stance on the issue, the Kingdom of Arendelle no longer does business with *Weasle*ton.

MORNING AT ARENDELLE CASTLE

It's another busy morning at Arendelle Castle. Every morning, the staff prepares for the day's activities, sometimes even before the sun rises! Since there's always something to celebrate in the Kingdom of Arendelle, the staff needs to make sure everything runs smoothly. Olina and her staff wake up early to begin preparing breakfast and the rest of the day's meals while Kai lights all of the candles and surveys each room to make sure nothing is out of place.

Elsa enjoys attending to her queenly duties early in the morning, that way she can better prepare herself for the day ahead. Anna, on the other hand, prefers to sleep in, which is quite an accomplishment since she lives in a bustling castle!

Gerda is receiving the morning's fresh flower delivery. The colourful blooms give the castle extra cheer.

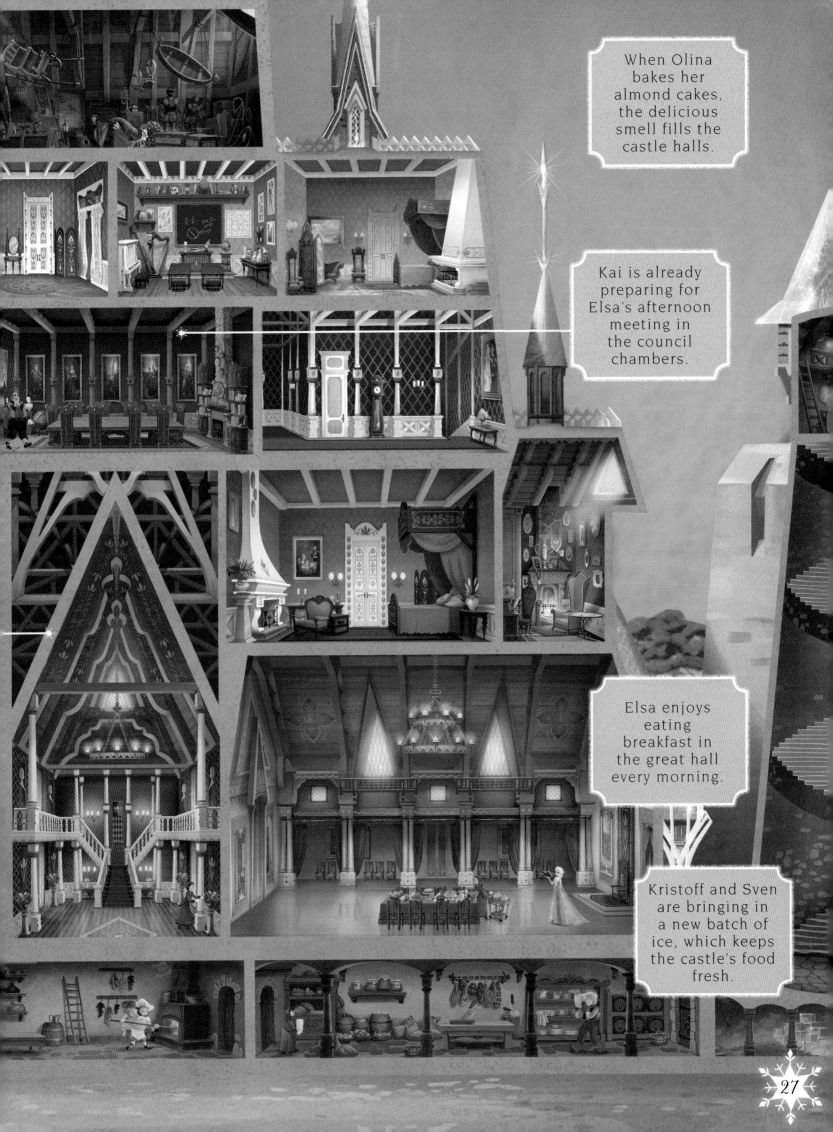

When Olina bakes her almond cakes, the delicious smell fills the castle halls.

Kai is already preparing for Elsa's afternoon meeting in the council chambers.

Elsa enjoys eating breakfast in the great hall every morning.

Kristoff and Sven are bringing in a new batch of ice, which keeps the castle's food fresh.

THE GREAT HALL

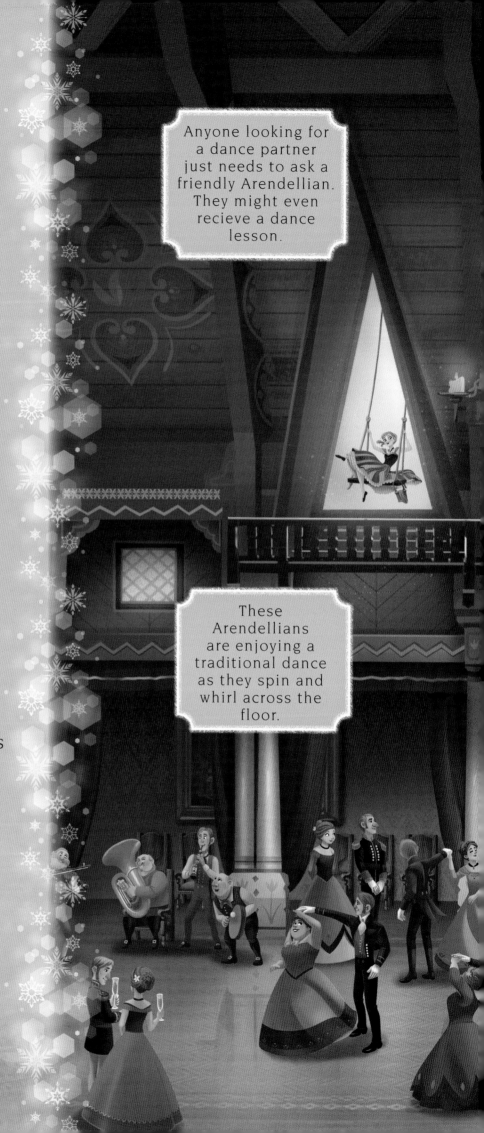

From birthday celebrations to more reserved, traditional events, over the years the great hall has hosted many festive, memorable occasions. When an event is held in the great hall, laughter can be heard throughout the castle and a good time is had by all. A typical event in the great hall includes a live band playing traditional Arendellian music, special food and beverages for guests to enjoy and, of course, lots of dancing!

Preparations for more elaborate occasions occur several days in advance. The floor must be polished, the curtains steamed and each candle on the golden chandelier must be lit. Depending on the guest count, Olina and her staff receive several food deliveries and can spend up to three days preparing a full feast. Tonight, Elsa has invited some guests to enjoy the latest Arendellian delicacies and dance the night away!

Anyone looking for a dance partner just needs to ask a friendly Arendellian. They might even recieve a dance lesson.

These Arendellians are enjoying a traditional dance as they spin and whirl across the floor.

The triangular windows allow for plenty of natural lighting during the daytime.

These two balconies are a perfect place for tired dancers to take a break and rest their feet.

Elsa's throne is rarely used except for formal occasions.

THE SECOND GREAT HALL

The second great hall is one of the tallest rooms in the castle.

These official banners of Arendelle change with each new season.

Located at the centre of the castle, the second great hall is perfect for greeting guests and making a grand entrance worthy of royalty. Visitors are impressed as they step through the glass doors and are greeted with gold-trimmed walls, a grand staircase and soaring wooden ceilings. One of the official banners of Arendelle is displayed proudly at the centre of the room with additional decorative banners featuring Elsa's silhouette and the crocus, the official flower of Arendelle, on the sides. Gerda likes filling this entry room with fresh flowers so guests feel welcome as soon as they walk inside the castle. Every candle is kept lit throughout the day in case unexpected visitors should arrive.

During springtime the doors are kept open, filling the room with crisp Arendellian air.

When Elsa performs her queenly duties, she greets guests in this room.

These glass doors lead to the great hall.

The staircase may look formal, but Anna has been known to slide down the banisters!

ANNA'S BEDROOM

Anna's rose-coloured room is bright and cheery, just like her! Her bedroom is one of her favourite places in the castle and she can often be found there writing letters or hanging out with her friends. At night, she loves snuggling up under her soft duvet with a good book before she falls asleep. She keeps a chest nearby full of her favourite stories and cosiest blankets.

The heavy fabric around her bed helps block out the sun on days when she'd like to get a little extra shut eye – which is most days. Every morning, Kai gently knocks on Anna's door to wake her, though it may take a few extra knocks and a bit of persuasion to convince her to get out of bed. But once she wipes the sleep from her eyes, she hops out of bed and is ready to greet whatever new adventure awaits her!

During chilly winter nights, Anna likes to keep warm by the fireplace, which is stocked with plenty of firewood.

This painting
of Arendelle
is one of
Anna's
favourites.

The decorative
carpets help
keep Anna's feet
warm when she
can't find her
slippers.

Anna is going
to read this
book next.

33

ELSA'S BEDROOM

Although they once shared a bedroom, Elsa moved to her own room after she accidentally struck Anna with her powers. As a child, Elsa spent many days alone in her bedroom, so she really made it her own. She would pass the time reading her favourite books, writing in her diary, and trying her best not to unleash her powers. Even though she felt isolated, she was never too far from Anna – her bedroom was just down the hallway with only the schoolroom and the dressing room separating them.

Over the years, Elsa updated her bedroom to a luxurious purple and blue retreat. Her elegant bed, filled with down feathers for extra comfort had a canopy covering, which made it very snug. Every morning when she woke up, she would look at the painting of Arendelle Castle to remind herself of her queenly duties and the people she promised to serve and protect. She also loved looking at the painting of her ice palace – it encouraged her to stay true to herself.

After she returned to Arendelle and restored summer, Elsa moved into her parents' room, which helped to give her a fresh start, although she still loves spending time in her childhood bedroom.

Snowflake details like this one on Elsa's rug reflect her unique powers.

Gerda makes sure to keep fresh flowers by the bedside. They remind Elsa of the outdoors and her freedom.

When Anna stops by to spend time with her sister, she usually sits on Elsa's bed.

Elsa likes writing about her day in her diary.

THE DRESSING ROOM

Elsa and Anna have a variety of clothes and accessories, so they always have the perfect outfit for all of their different adventures! From royal gowns to heavy cloaks, regal ceremonial sashes, sun hats and sleighing gear, this room holds an outfit for every occasion. As children, the sisters used to play dress-up in this room, trying on anything from their father's ceremonial capes and their mother's scarves to helmets and armour.

All of Anna and Elsa's outfits are handmade and tailored to their exact measurements and crafted from the finest materials. Once the seamstress makes a piece of clothing, the item is sent to the best embroiderer in Arendelle who adds intricate details.

Elsa and Anna try on their outfits behind this elegant dressing screen.

Anna is about to give her outfit one final look in the mirror before heading off on an adventure with Kristoff.

This upper storage compartment is where Anna and Elsa keep their hats and shoes.

Gerda keeps the dressing room organised and swaps out the appropriate clothing based on each season.

37

THE PORTRAIT GALLERY

The portrait gallery holds a lot of important memories for the Kingdom of Arendelle and many pieces of beautiful artwork. It took the artists several months to complete each painting in this room that captures a special moment in time. Some of the paintings are of Anna and Elsa's relatives while others capture classic snapshots of Arendellian history.

When Anna was younger, the paintings in the portrait gallery offered a glimpse of the outside world and the potential future she could have once the castle gates were opened. She especially liked picturing herself being pushed on the swing and enjoying a relaxing outdoor picnic. She also imagined what each person was thinking while they were posing for their portrait. Sometimes she would go to the library to find out more about the people in the paintings like their name, their history and what they liked to do for fun.

Anna knows very little about these two statue busts except that they are very, very heavy.

Anna and Elsa's favourite painting is this portrait of them with their parents.

This painting of Anna and Elsa's father reminds Elsa of her queenly responsibilities.

Sven enjoys visiting the portrait gallery from time to time. Maybe one day there will be a portrait of a reindeer proudly displayed!

THE LIBRARY

Anna and Elsa love scanning the shelves in the library for stories that spark their imaginations. These bookshelves hold everything from Arendellian history to whimsical fairy tales and stories from local authors and ancient times. And if a curious mind ever needs information on the fjord, there is an entire section dedicated to the science of fjord creation.

Elsa will sometimes reference the historical books located on these shelves to assist her in making thoughtful decisions for her kingdom. The time Anna spent in the library as a child helped to fuel her vivid imagination. She also loved telling made up stories to anyone who would listen, including the portraits hanging on the wall. Ever since Olaf learned to read, he enjoys perusing the philosophy books and discovering more about the world around him.

Each book is handmade and written by a skilled letterer.

If anyone accidentally locks the door, Olaf can use his nose as a key – it fits perfectly inside the keyhole.

This shelf holds the book that led King Agnarr and his family to the Valley of the Living Rock when Elsa accidentally struck Anna with her magic.

This fireplace is made of stone sourced from the nearby mountains.

THE ATTIC

Located at the very top of Arendelle Castle, the attic is where Anna and Elsa keep some of their most important possessions. The attic also stores a lot of active gear, from bicycles to a variety of sleighs (for every different type of snow) and even row boats! Once every few years, Anna will come upstairs and peruse the items in the attic until she's unearthed a family treasure or found a new potential hobby. Maybe today she'll finally learn how to play the harp!

During sleepovers, the attic is the perfect place to tell silly ghost stories after dark. And if someone is looking for a place to hide during a competitive game of hide-and-seek, the attic is the place to go.

This sleigh is one of the fastest in the kingdom.

THE COUNCIL CHAMBERS

The wooden table in the council chambers has been present for several generations of Arendellian policy and decision making. From drafting new trade agreements with foreign countries to signing thank you cards, Elsa believes no task is too big or small for this room. Even though the décor of the council chambers sets a formal tone, and the portraits are certainly stoic, there are a few playful rosemaling details throughout the room on the chairs, cabinet and carpet. Rosemaling is a traditional form of Arendellian decorative art that can be seen throughout the castle.

When there are disagreements in Arendelle, Elsa invites both parties to settle matters in the council chambers. Though, if discussions get too intense, Kai and Gerda are always on standby with delicious treats to try to ease tensions.

Important papers are stored inside this globe, which has a secret compartment.

Elsa is signing an important document that took many weeks to draft.

When Anna and Elsa were much smaller, they liked to play underneath the table.

Kai and Gerda hung these artistic shields to brighten up the décor of the room while also serving as a reminder of Arendelle's history.

These chairs are just as uncomfortable as they look – it encourages faster decision making.

These books hold the Arendellian kingdom's records and laws.

Sven knows he will always find a supply of fresh carrots in the kitchen!

The kitchen does not have a refrigerator. The food is stored nearby in an ice cellar that Kristoff keeps stocked.

THE
KITCHEN

From tasty treats to elegant feasts fit for royalty, the kitchen at Arendelle Castle has it covered! If someone is looking for an authentic Arendellian meal, they need to look no farther than the kitchen.

All of the ingredients are sourced from Arendellian farmers and the recipes go

During Arendellian winters, the kitchen is one of the warmest places in the house thanks to this wood-burning oven.

This pastry chef is making the crust for Anna's favourite chocolate pie.

This baker is almost finished baking the bread for tomorrow's breakfast.

back several generations, with some modern refinements, of course.

Anna and Elsa can request almost anything from the kitchen, the staff is always delighted to see a smile on their faces. As long as they don't ask Olina for her secret triple chocolate chip cookie recipe – she will never give it up!

The kitchen staff cook all of the meals for Arendelle Castle and supply the food and beverages for special events like balls, banquets and birthdays. In addition to all of the meals, the kitchen always has snacks on hand for when Anna and Elsa are looking for a special treat.

THE CHAPEL

The chapel is where most of the official Arendellian ceremonies take place. Other formal events such as weddings and coronations – a formal ceremony where the new ruler is crowned – take place here as well. People from Arendelle and royals from faraway kingdoms attend these events, which are typically followed by an elaborate celebration in the great hall.

The bell tower is the highest point in the chapel as well as one of the tallest structures in the kingdom. If anyone climbs the stairs leading to the singular bell at the top, they will have to go alone – there's only enough room for one person to fit at a time. The bell is rung for a variety of different reasons including days of celebration.

These stained-glass windows were handmade by Arendellian glass makers.

Reserved for the priest, this chair dates back several centuries.

This bell is the original from when the tower was first built.

As children, Anna and Elsa loved to race up the bell tower stairs.

Villagers, like this family, often come to the chapel to meet with the priest.

NIGHTTIME AT ARENDELLE CASTLE

It's been an eventful day filled with fun and adventure at Arendelle Castle. Now that the sun has set, it's time for the castle staff to make preparations for the evening. First, the castle gates are closed to outside visitors and each room is cleaned up from that day's events. Next, Kai extinguishes all of the candles in the same order as the previous night... and every night before that.

When Anna and Elsa were younger, they used to try to stay up late each night. Their parents would often find them sneaking bedtime snacks from the kitchen. Now the sisters like to wind down after a long day in the library, reading their favourite stories, playing games like charades and sharing their favourite parts of their day. Once they feel their eyelids starting to get heavy, Anna and Elsa make their way to their bedrooms and curl up under the covers.

On chilly nights, the fireplaces are lit and maintained to keep the castle warm.

Sometimes, when Kristoff has finished his nighttime reading, he'll play his lute.

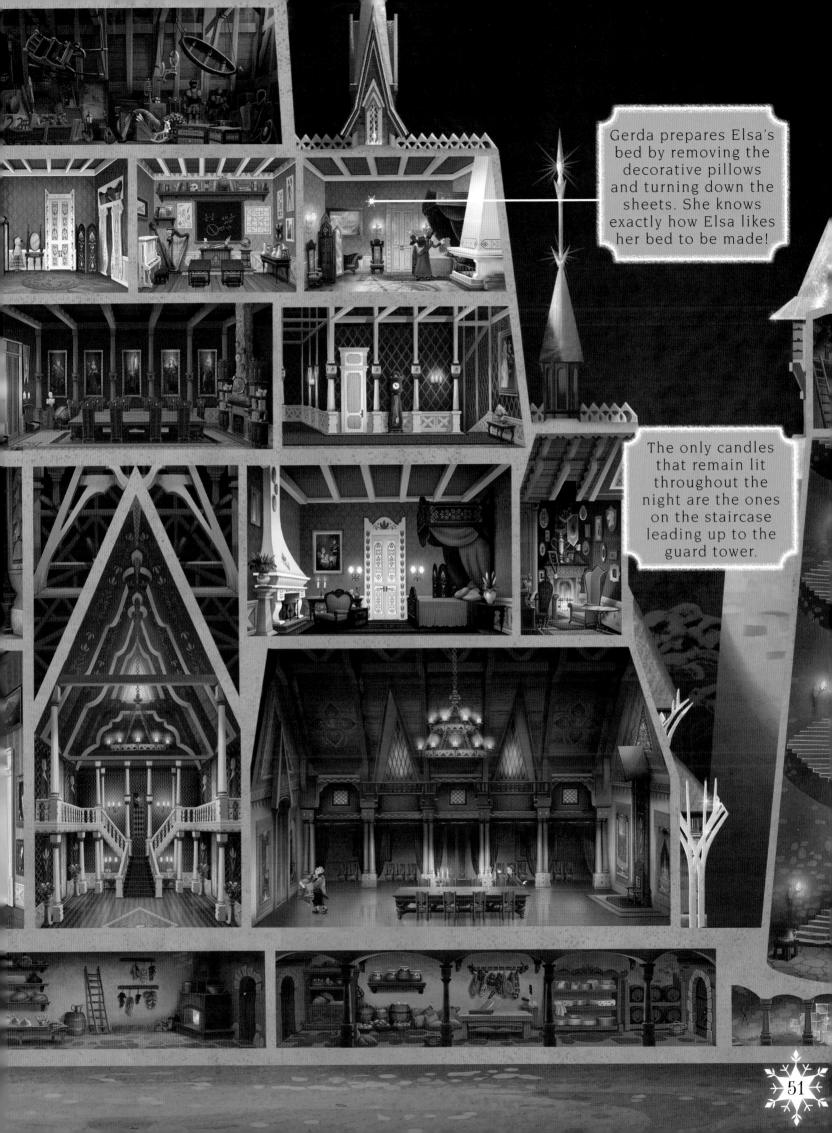

Gerda prepares Elsa's bed by removing the decorative pillows and turning down the sheets. She knows exactly how Elsa likes her bed to be made!

The only candles that remain lit throughout the night are the ones on the staircase leading up to the guard tower.

ARENDELLE CASTLE COURTYARD

The castle courtyard is one of the main marketplaces where the best vendors from Arendelle Village are invited to sell their goods. From exquisite textiles to fresh produce, anyone can find whatever they may need if they look closely enough!

During spring and summer, the castle courtyard is filled with flower vendors offering everything from special crocus seeds to elaborate wildflower bouquets. In the warmer months, vendors sell fresh strawberries, lingonberries and Morello cherries. And the winter market offerings are not to be underestimated – holiday cookies and hot chocolate are among the most popular items.

One of the most exciting times of year for the Kingdom of Arendelle is the end of harvest season. Elsa and Anna host a community meal featuring foods made from that year's harvest.

On most days, seagulls can be found roaming the skies, looking to swoop down and sneak a tasty treat.

When Anna visits the castle courtyard, she checks in with each vendor to see how they are doing.

With the fjord just outside these walls, fresh fish deliveries arrive daily.

If it's a slow day at the castle, Olina will provide a special treat for villagers to enjoy!

The castle staff hung these flower garlands for a community celebration taking place tonight.

ARENDELLE CASTLE STABLES

These empty stables are for visitors who arrive at the castle on horseback.

The stables are where Anna's horse Havski lives. Every morning after breakfast, Anna heads down to the stables to visit with her horse and take him out for a ride. She loves feeling the fresh Arendellian breeze on her face and feeling connected with the kingdom, and her horse loves it, too. When she returns to the stable, Anna's horse, and any other horses that may be visiting the stables, are given a royal grooming session complete with a brushing.

The stables are stocked daily with bales of hay, fresh water and special treats like carrots and apples, although Sven has been known to sneak a few carrots from this stash. Aside from providing lodging for the horses, the stables also hold all of the equestrian equipment from saddles to stirrups, bridles and blankets.

This horse is visiting for the day while his rider attends to matters at the castle.

Anna has decided to go on her morning ride. Time to saddle up!

Olaf likes visiting Havski at the stables. They have a lot to talk about (well, mostly Olaf does).

Sven and Kristoff will sometimes come to the stables for some peace and quiet.

WHO'S WHO
ARENDELLE AND BEYOND

OAKEN is the owner of Oaken's Trading Post and Sauna. Aside from being a business owner, Oaken is a bit of an inventor and sells his creations exclusively at his store. During his large family reunions, Oaken's favourite activity is the Creators Contest where each family member shows off their own invention!

MARSHMALLOW was created by Elsa when she wanted Anna and Kristoff to leave her ice palace. With a thunderous roar, Marshmallow chased them out of the castle and through the snowy forest. From that point on, Marshmallow has guarded the ice palace from unwanted visitors, offering a pretty scary sight for unsuspecting guests.

GRAND PABBIE is a wise troll who helped cure Anna when Elsa accidentally struck her with magic as a child. He also examined Anna after Elsa's magic struck her in the heart and explained that only an act of true love could save her. Several years later, he advised Elsa to go to the Enchanted Forest after her magic awoke the spirits of nature.

BULDA is the matriarch of the troll family and considers herself a bit of a love expert. She first met Kristoff and Sven when they were very young and she has been looking after them ever since. Each crystal on her necklace holds a special meaning. Her favourite is the one Grand Pabbie gave her when she adopted Kristoff and Sven.

LITTLE ROCK may look like a moss-covered boulder at first, but there's more to him than meets the eye. A young, rambunctious troll with a creative imagination, this sweet little guy loves waking up to the Northern Lights and dreaming about what new adventure awaits him.

ARENDELLE VILLAGE

Just outside the main entrance to Arendelle Castle lies Arendelle Village, home to the people Elsa serves as queen. The quaint, rustic village has restaurants, homes, parks, a variety of speciality shops, a library and a school. Every day after school, the children play outdoors. Sometimes their joyful voices can be heard from the castle.

Anna enjoys spending time in Arendelle Village and connecting with the people who live there. Everyone in Arendelle Village has a story, and Anna has heard all of them – at least twice! Sometimes, she likes to visit the local library where she enjoys perusing the shelves.

Elsa always enjoys the time she spends in Arendelle Village and she loves to help the people of Arendelle. Although her queenly duties keep her busy at the castle, she always tries to make a visit to the village when her schedule permits.

Though the buildings in the village share a similar design, different paints provide a pop of colour.

In winter, children enjoy skating outside the castle gates after school!

58

OAKEN'S
TRADING POST & SAUNA

Oaken's Trading Post and Sauna sells a variety of goods including fresh food, fashionable apparel and equipment for mountain adventures. An inventor at heart, Oaken also sells a selection of his own creations including cough remedies, snow shoes and sun balm. He always wants his customers leaving his shop with "good feelings," so if a customer is unsatisfied with their experience, he will throw in a free quart of lutefisk or a free sauna experience.

At night, the single trail of smoke pouring out of the top of Oaken's shop attracts visitors. When potential customers get closer, a warm glow comes from inside the shop, inviting visitors to walk up the stone steps that lead to the wooden front porch. When Anna went searching for Elsa after she fled Arendelle, she was so relieved when she saw the smoke from Oaken's shop rising into the sky. Soon after she arrived, a snow-covered man entered the shop – it was Kristoff.

Customers planning to visit the sauna should do so before Oaken's large family does, otherwise they may have to wait a while.

WARM CAPES

SUPPLIES

SALE

If you're looking for a deal, Oaken has a Big Blowout sale each season.

BIG WINTER BLOWOUT

When customers step inside Oaken's Trading Post and Sauna, they'll likely be greeted with the sound of Oaken's signature "Hoo, hoo"!

These bottles are filled with Oaken's creations, exclusively available for sale at his shop.

SPECIALITIES

This counter is where customers pay for their goods, but when the shop is closed, Oaken uses it as his invention desk.

Oaken stocks extra winter gear in case an unexpected winter comes in summer... again.

ELSA'S ICE PALACE EXTERIOR

When Elsa fled Arendelle after her powers were accidentally revealed, she headed towards the North Mountain. Once she arrived, Elsa removed her glove and began exploring the full extent of her powers, something she had never done before. After Elsa created a few snowflake swirls and unknowingly formed Olaf again, she began constructing the ice palace. The ice palace was the product of Elsa finally being able to express her true self and unleash her powers. It would be the first place where Elsa felt entirely free.

Elsa began constructing the ice palace with the creation of the outdoor staircase and railings that connected two sides of a gorge. Then, with a stomp of her foot, she used her powers to build the foundation of the palace into the peak of the North Mountain. From that foundation, the walls quickly came together with intricate snowflake details.

Marshmallow still guards the castle's entrance from any unwanted visitors.

These spires inspired Elsa's icy redesign of Arendelle Castle.

Unlike her bedroom in the castle, the ice palace has many windows and open balconies.

The North Mountain is far from Arendelle, making the ice palace a remote destination.

On his first visit to the ice palace, Sven got his tongue stuck on the staircase railing.

ELSA'S ICE PALACE INTERIOR

Every inch of the interior of Elsa's ice palace is designed to Elsa's preferences, from the reflective ice flooring to the sparkling grand chandelier. When she first created the ice palace, the interior details seemed to flow from Elsa, though if there was ever something she wanted to change in the future, she could change it instantly with a bit of magic.

Since the palace is connected to Elsa's powers, when her emotions change, sometimes the inside of the palace reflects her mood by forming more ice crystals or changing colour. Although the ice palace offered Elsa a place of comfort and release during her departure from Arendelle, it is also the site of less tranquil moments like when Elsa struck Anna in the heart and Hans and the other guards took Elsa prisoner.

When Anna first walked through the front doors, this arched stairway was the first thing she saw.

The smooth, slippery ice floor may feel cold to some, but it doesn't bother Elsa.

Tall ceilings allow Elsa to explore her magic indoors, without limits.

Various shades of blue and purple are featured prominently throughout the ice palace.

These intricate designs look similar to the rosemaling details found in the castle, with an icy twist.

VALLEY OF THE LIVING ROCK

A short journey north from Arendelle Village lies the Valley of the Living Rock, home to Grand Pabbie, Bulda and the rest of the trolls. During the day, Valley of the Living Rock might seem like a deserted part of the forest, but once nightfall comes, and the trolls roll out of their rock disguises, it's full of laughter and activity. Having grown up in the Valley of the Living Rock, Kristoff and Sven feel right at home among the rambunctious trolls, though they might seem a bit overwhelming to outsiders.

Tonight, everyone is preparing for Kristoff's adoptive father Cliff's surprise century party (trolls only celebrate birthdays every hundred years). There's sure to be plenty of mud pie to go around. It may sound gross, but mud pie is actually a delicious troll delicacy. There will be bat races, a scavenger hunt for crystals and troll bowling, a game which involves a troll rolling down a hill into a stack of pinecones.

There's plenty of hugs to go around in the Valley of the Living Rock.

The Valley of the Living Rock is one of the best places to view the Northern Lights.

Both times when Anna was struck with magic, she was brought to the Valley of the Living Rock in search of a cure.

Bulda always carries extra snacks for Sven.

WHO'S WHO
NORTH OF ARENDELLE

LIEUTENANT MATTIAS, who served as Anna and Elsa's father's official guard, has spent over 34 years trapped inside the Enchanted Forest. When Anna meets him in the Enchanted Forest, she recognises Mattias from his portrait, which hangs in the library inside Arendelle Castle.

YELANA, a strong Northuldra woman whose preferred weapon is a staff, is the leader of the Northuldra people. At first she doesn't believe nature would reward Elsa, an Arendellian, with magical powers, but she can't deny that Elsa is the reason the spirits of nature are visiting the Northuldra camp.

HONEYMAREN is a young Northuldra woman who shares her knowledge with Elsa. She points out the symbols of nature on Elsa's mother's scarf including the symbol of the bridge. Honeymaren explains that the day the forest fell, the bridge cried out to the spirits, turning them against everyone in the forest.

RYDER, Honeymaren's brother, is a skilled reindeer herder. He quickly connects with Kristoff given their shared appreciation for the majestic creatures. When the Fire Spirit threatens the herd, Ryder and Kristoff team up to heroically lead the reindeer away from the flames and to safety.

BRUNI, the Fire Spirit is one of the spirits of nature, which includes the Wind Spirit, the Water Spirit, and the Earth Giants. The Fire Spirit may seem scary, but once it cools off, it takes the form of an adorable, playful salamander. Although one of Bruni's blasts can instantly ignite a tree, Elsa realises that the Fire Spirit is more scared than intentionally destructive and treats it to some snowflake snacks.

THE MONOLITHS

On the outskirts of the Enchanted Forest stand four giant monoliths, each representing the four spirits of nature – fire, water, wind and earth. When Anna and Elsa arrive at the mist guarding the Enchanted Forest, they hold hands and the mist magically rolls in on itself before them. As the mist parts, in front of them stand the four towering grey monoliths. Close behind the sisters follow Kristoff, Olaf and Sven who also admire the breathtaking sight.

Few have seen the monoliths since the mist rose up surrounding the Enchanted Forest and no one in the group has encountered a sight quite like this before. But their time in front of the monoliths quickly comes to an end when the mist starts to powerfully shove them until they are forced to run deeper into the mist – and the unknown.

The Monoliths are made of stone from the local mountains and have stood for several generations.

Each of the symbols specifically represents one of the four spirits of nature.

The Monoliths stand just inside the magical mist that keeps visitors out of the Enchanted Forest.

The Monoliths are about four times the height of Elsa.

Each monolith is entirely unique in shape and design except for the diamond shape and triangular carved details.

The Arendelle Dam was built under orders from Anna and Elsa's grandfather, King Runeard.

This stream feeds the fjord that surrounds Arendelle Castle.

THE ENCHANTED FOREST

The Enchanted Forest, a mysterious place Anna and Elsa's father mentioned when he told them a bedtime story about the night the forest fell, is surrounded by a magical mist that encases the forest, not allowing outsiders in, or the people trapped inside to leave. When the elements leave Arendelle, Grand Pabbie advises Elsa and Anna to

If someone feels a gust of wind blowing, they should look out! It may be Gale, the Wind Spirit.

When Olaf ran through this star moss he quickly became covered in it.

When Olaf looks down into this brook, the Water Nokk looks back up at him from below.

set out in search of the Enchanted Forest to discover why the mysterious kulning voice is calling to Elsa and what it wants. When Anna, Elsa and their friends arrive at the mist, they notice it rolls in on itself and that if they try to penetrate it, they bounce off like balloons. Luckily, the mist parts when Anna and Elsa hold hands, allowing the group to enter.

Once an outsider passes through the mist, the Enchanted Forest offers a sight unlike anything else they've ever seen. It is mesmerising with soft rays of light that appear through the colourful leaves. The Enchanted Forest is also home to the majestic Arendelle Dam, which protects Arendelle from flooding.

The crocus, the official flower of Arendelle, appears on this flag.

IDUNA AND AGNARR'S SHIP

Surrounded by a fjord, sea travel is one of the main modes of transportation for Arendelle. When Elsa's powers were only growing stronger, her parents set out on their ship to search for answers to help Elsa. The journey was only supposed to last two weeks, but sadly Iduna and Agnarr's ship was overtaken by strong, violent waves during a storm.

This ship offered a stunning view from the balcony at the bow, or front, of the ship.

Anna and Elsa are surprised to see their parents' ship in the north rather than in the Southern Sea.

The final location of their parents' ship remained a mystery until Elsa followed the kulning sound, which led her farther north and she happened upon the wreckage.

When Elsa and Anna found the ship wreckage and started exploring the ruins, Anna discovered a notch in the floor containing a small glass tube, sealed with a cork. Inside were some pieces of parchment that contained information about her parents' final voyage.

Among the pieces of parchment was a map to Ahtohallan, the secret river her mother had told her and Elsa about when they were children. The river is said to hold the answers to the past.

THE DARK SEA

Acting as a barrier protecting Ahtohallan from the outside world, the Dark Sea is a tumultuous body of water that few are powerful enough to pass through. Elsa's initial attempts to cross are unsuccessful and she is repeatedly tossed under the waves and returned back to the shore. Even her daring attempt to travel above the waves, by creating ice floats to jump on top of, does not work.

The Dark Sea is home to the Water Nokk, one of the spirits of nature whose power is both threatening and spectacular. When Elsa attempts to cross the Dark Sea to get to Ahtohallan, she sees the Water Nokk springing up from the depths straight for her. After spending time struggling with the Water Nokk, Elsa gets the idea to create an ice bridle that hooks around the horse's mouth and nose. Once she swings onto its back, they move together straight for Ahtohallan.

On one of Elsa's attempts to cross the Dark Sea, she climbs to the top of these cliffs and creates an ice slide.

These high waves and dark waters pose a challenge for even the most skilled swimmer.

At night, lightning storms frequently light up the sky above the Dark Sea.

Across the Dark Sea, just beyond the shore, lies Ahtohallan.

Beneath the waves lies the Water Nokk. It could spring from the depths at any moment.